Preface

The landscape of Indian accounting is undergoing a dynamic shift. The familiar realm of manual ledgers and desktop software is rapidly evolving to embrace the transformative power of cloud-based solutions. This book, "Empowering the Indian Chartered Accountants: A Comprehensive Guide to Conquering the Cloud-Accounting Era," serves as your compass on this exciting journey.

As a Chartered Accountant (CA) in India, you are uniquely positioned to leverage this digital revolution. Cloud accounting unlocks a treasure trove of benefits, empowering you to streamline workflows, enhance client service offerings, and navigate the ever-changing financial landscape with greater efficiency and agility.

This book is designed to be your one-stop guide to mastering cloud accounting. We delve into the heart of the matter, exploring the limitations of traditional accounting practices and the compelling reasons for embracing the cloud. We unpack the core concepts of cloud accounting, highlighting the advantages it offers, from cost-effectiveness and real-

time data management to seamless collaboration and improved accessibility.

Moving beyond the fundamentals, we delve into the evolving role of the CA in the cloud era. We explore how cloud accounting empowers you to streamline workflows, automate tedious tasks, and offer your clients a broader range of value-added services. We equip you with strategies for client acquisition and growth, allowing you to position yourself as a thought leader in the digital accounting space.

However, the path to cloud adoption isn't always without its challenges. We dedicate a section to addressing potential concerns in the Indian context, such as data security, internet connectivity issues, and integration challenges. We provide practical mitigation strategies to ensure a smooth and successful transition.

Finally, we recognize the importance of navigating the regulatory environment. We offer guidance on ensuring compliance with data residency regulations and staying updated on any relevant changes.

This book is your comprehensive resource for unlocking the full potential of cloud accounting in your practice. Whether you are a seasoned CA or just embarking on your career journey, this guide equips you with the knowledge and strategies to thrive in the dynamic world of cloud-based accounting.

Welcome to the future of Indian accounting – embrace the cloud and empower your practice to soar!

Acknowledgments

Writing this book on Cloud Accounting in the Indian Accounting Landscape has been an enriching experience. It would not have been possible without the support and contributions of many individuals.

First and foremost, I want to express my sincere gratitude to the countless practicing Chartered Accountants whose dedication and commitment inspire me. Their tireless efforts and willingness to adapt are driving the evolution of the accounting profession in India.

A special debt of thanks goes to **Priyanka Sharma** my wife and support system and **Aarush Sharma** my son for their invaluable insights, constructive criticism, and unwavering encouragement throughout the writing process. Your expertise and guidance significantly shaped the content and direction of this book.

I am also grateful to the developers and innovators behind the various cloud accounting platforms for their dedication to building cutting-edge solutions that empower accounting professionals.

Finally, I extend my heartfelt appreciation to my family and friends especially **Ankit Aggarwal,** my younger brother for their unwavering support during the creation of this book.

This book is a testament to the collective knowledge and collaborative spirit of the Indian accounting community. May it serve as a valuable resource for all Chartered Accountants embarking on their cloud accounting journey.

Thank You...
CA. Peeyush Sharma
peeyushsharmaca@gmail.com

The Indian accounting landscape is undergoing a significant transformation. Traditional practices are giving way to the power and convenience of cloud technology. This book, *"Cloud Accounting in the Indian Accounting Landscape,"* serves as your guide to navigating this exciting new frontier.

My purpose in writing this book is twofold. Firstly, I want to equip practicing Chartered Accountants with the knowledge and tools necessary to embrace cloud accounting. Secondly, I aim to illuminate the vast potential of this technology for streamlining workflows, enhancing client service, and propelling your practice towards new heights.

Throughout these pages, we will delve into the core concepts of cloud accounting, exploring its evolution, advantages, and potential challenges. We'll then analyze the current state of Indian accounting, highlighting the limitations of traditional methods and the urgent need for technological integration.

The heart of the book delves into the key features and benefits of cloud accounting. We'll explore how real-time collaboration, unparalleled accessibility, robust security measures, and seamless integration with other business tools can revolutionize your practice. We'll also examine popular cloud accounting platforms available in India, providing comparisons to help you choose the perfect solution.

Transitioning to cloud accounting requires careful planning. This book offers a step-by-step guide for implementing the technology in your practice, addressing potential resistance from team members, and fostering a culture of continuous learning.

Ultimately, this book is an advocate for the transformative power of cloud accounting. By adopting this technology, Chartered Accountants can unlock a new level of efficiency, strengthen client relationships, generate significant cost savings, and propel their practices towards unparalleled growth.

Join me on this journey to explore real-world case studies, delve into regulatory considerations and security concerns, and unveil the exciting future trends shaping the landscape of cloud accounting in India.

Embrace the cloud, empower your practice, and soar with the future of Indian accounting!

CA. Peeyush Sharma
18th May, 2024

Table of Contents

This book aims to provide a comprehensive guide for practicing Chartered Accountants in India, exploring the transformative impact of cloud accounting on their profession. Through practical insights, Case studies, and a thorough examination of key platforms, the book will empower accountants to embrace technology, streamline their processes, and enhance their role in the rapidly evolving Indian accounting landscape.

1

Introduction

In the dynamic landscape of modern accounting, the advent of cloud technology has ushered in a transformative era for professionals and businesses alike. The traditional methods of accounting, laden with manual processes and constrained by physical limitations, are gradually giving way to the efficiency and agility offered by cloud accounting. In the Indian context, where the accounting profession plays a pivotal role in the economic ecosystem, embracing cloud technology is not just a choice but a strategic imperative.

1.1 Background

The Indian accounting landscape, marked by its rich tapestry of businesses ranging from small enterprises to large corporations, has witnessed significant shifts in recent years. As the complexities of financial transactions grow, so does the demand for more streamlined, accurate, and real-time accounting solutions. The traditional pen-and-paper approach, though venerable, is proving insufficient to meet the dynamic requirements of the modern business environment.

The advent of cloud accounting, with its virtual infrastructure and collaborative capabilities, presents a compelling solution to the challenges faced by Chartered Accountants in India. Cloud accounting transcends geographical boundaries, providing unprecedented access to financial data, enabling real-time collaboration, and offering a level of security and scalability previously unimaginable.

1.2 Purpose of the Book

The purpose of this book is to serve as a guide and companion for practicing Chartered Accountants navigating the transformative landscape of cloud accounting in India. We aim to demystify the intricacies of cloud technology, explore its diverse applications in accounting, and equip professionals with the knowledge and tools needed to harness its full potential.

By delving into the nuances of cloud accounting platforms, addressing implementation challenges, and showcasing real-world Case studies, this book seeks to empower

Chartered Accountants to not only adapt to change but to thrive in an era where technology is reshaping the very fabric of their profession.

1.3 Scope and Importance of Cloud Accounting in India

Cloud accounting has emerged as a game-changer for businesses of all sizes in India, offering a multitude of benefits and a vast scope for transforming how financial data is managed. Here's a breakdown of its significance:

Scope of Cloud Accounting in India:

- **Accessibility and Scalability:** Cloud accounting solutions are accessible from anywhere with an internet connection, allowing remote work, collaboration, and real-time data access for businesses spread across locations. This is particularly beneficial for geographically dispersed Indian companies and those with a mobile workforce.

- **Cost-Effectiveness:** Cloud accounting eliminates the need for expensive hardware and software installations, IT maintenance, and dedicated IT staff.

This translates to significant cost savings for Indian businesses, especially for startups and SMEs with limited budgets.

- **Enhanced Security:** Cloud service providers invest heavily in robust security measures to protect sensitive financial data. Automatic backups and disaster recovery features offer peace of mind compared to traditional on-premise accounting systems.

- **Improved Collaboration:** Cloud accounting platforms facilitate seamless collaboration between accountants, bookkeepers, and business owners. Real-time data access and shared ledgers streamline communication and enhance financial transparency.

- **Integration with Business Applications:** Cloud accounting software integrates seamlessly with other business applications like CRM, inventory management, and e-commerce platforms, automating workflows and improving operational efficiency.

- **Regulatory Compliance:** Cloud accounting software can be updated automatically with the latest tax regulations in India, ensuring compliance and reducing the risk of errors or penalties.

- **Data Analytics and Business Insights:** Cloud accounting solutions offer built-in data analytics tools that provide valuable insights into financial performance, cash flow, and key metrics. This empowers Indian businesses to make data-driven decisions for growth.

Importance of Cloud Accounting in India:

The Indian economy is experiencing rapid growth, with a burgeoning number of SMEs and startups. Cloud accounting caters perfectly to their needs by:

- **Facilitating Business Growth:** Scalable and cost-effective solutions enable Indian businesses to manage their finances efficiently during periods of expansion.

- **Boosting Financial Transparency:** Real-time access to financial data empowers business owners to make informed decisions for better financial health.

- **Encouraging Entrepreneurship:** Reduced costs and simplified financial management make it easier for aspiring Indian entrepreneurs to launch and manage their businesses.

- **Supporting the Gig Economy:** Cloud accounting caters to the growing gig economy in India, allowing freelancers and independent contractors to manage their finances effectively.

- **Promoting Digital Transformation:** Cloud accounting is a stepping stone towards digital transformation, encouraging Indian businesses to embrace technology for improved efficiency.

The Indian government's initiatives like Digital India and Startup India further emphasize the importance of cloud adoption. Cloud accounting aligns perfectly with these goals by promoting paperless transactions, financial inclusion, and fostering a more tech-savvy business environment.

Cloud accounting offers a compelling value proposition for businesses of all sizes in India. Its vast scope and numerous benefits make it a crucial tool for streamlining financial management, promoting collaboration, and fostering business growth in the digital age. As India continues its economic journey, cloud accounting is poised to play a vital role in empowering businesses and entrepreneurs to achieve their financial goals.

2

Understanding Cloud Accounting: Your Financial Data in the Cloud

Imagine having access to your business's financial data anytime, anywhere, from any device. Cloud accounting makes this a reality, revolutionizing the way businesses manage their finances. But what exactly is cloud accounting, and how can it benefit your business?

What is Cloud Accounting?

Traditional accounting software involves installing programs on your computer. Cloud accounting, on the other hand, operates on remote servers accessed through the Internet. Think of it like storing your financial data in a secure online vault, accessible with a login and password.

Benefits of Cloud Accounting:

- **Accessibility:** Access your financial data anytime, anywhere, from any device with an internet connection. This is ideal for remote work, collaboration, and real-time financial insights.

- **Cost-Effectiveness:** Cloud accounting eliminates the need for expensive software installations, hardware upgrades, and dedicated IT staff. This translates to significant cost savings, especially for startups and small businesses.

- **Enhanced Security:** Cloud service providers invest heavily in robust security measures to safeguard your financial data. Automatic backups and disaster recovery features offer peace of mind compared to traditional on-premise accounting systems.

- **Improved Collaboration:** Cloud accounting platforms facilitate seamless collaboration between accountants, bookkeepers, and business owners. Real-time data access and shared ledgers streamline communication and financial transparency.

- **Integration with Business Applications:** Cloud accounting software integrates with other business applications like CRM, inventory management, and e-commerce platforms. This automates workflows and improves operational efficiency.

- **Automatic Updates:** Cloud accounting software updates automatically with the latest tax regulations, ensuring compliance and reducing the risk of errors or penalties.

- **Data Analytics and Insights:** Cloud solutions offer built-in data analytics tools that provide valuable insights into financial performance, cash flow, and key metrics. This empowers you to make data-driven decisions for business growth.

Is Cloud Accounting Right for You?

Cloud accounting is a great fit for businesses of all sizes, from startups and freelancers to established companies. Here are some factors to consider:

- **Size and Complexity of Your Business:** Cloud accounting is particularly beneficial for businesses that need remote access, collaboration features, and cost-effective solutions.

- **Technical Expertise:** Cloud accounting is user-friendly and requires minimal technical expertise. Most platforms offer intuitive interfaces and helpful tutorials.

- **Security Concerns:** Cloud service providers prioritize data security. However, it's crucial to choose a reputable provider with robust security measures.

Getting Started with Cloud Accounting:

- **Research Different Options:** There are numerous cloud accounting solutions available, each with its own features and pricing plans. Research popular options and choose one that aligns with your business needs and budget.

- **Migrate Your Data (Optional):** If you're using traditional accounting software, most cloud providers offer data migration services to seamlessly transfer your existing data.

- **Explore the Features:** Take advantage of free trials or demos offered by cloud accounting providers to familiarize yourself with the software's features and functionalities.

Cloud accounting offers a secure, accessible, and cost-effective way to manage your business finances. By embracing cloud technology, you can streamline financial processes, gain valuable insights, and empower your business for growth in the digital age.

2.1 Definition and Key Concepts

Definition:

Cloud accounting refers to the practice of utilizing internet-based computing resources to perform accounting functions, store financial data, and facilitate collaboration among stakeholders. Unlike traditional accounting software hosted on individual computers, cloud accounting operates on virtual servers, providing remote access to data and applications.

Key Concepts:

- *Virtualization:* Cloud accounting leverages virtualization technology, allowing for the creation of virtual servers, networks, and storage. This virtual environment enables seamless access to accounting applications and data from various devices connected to the internet.

- *Data Storage and Accessibility:* Centralized data storage on cloud servers ensures easy access to financial information from anywhere with an internet connection. This accessibility fosters real-time collaboration among multiple users, transcending geographical constraints.

- *Scalability:* Cloud accounting offers scalability to accommodate the evolving needs of businesses. Whether a small startup or a large enterprise, organizations can scale their computing resources up or down based on demand, optimizing costs and efficiency.

- *Subscription-Based Models:* Cloud accounting often follows a subscription-based model, eliminating the need for large upfront investments in software licenses and infrastructure. Users pay for services on a recurring basis, promoting cost-effectiveness and flexibility.

2.2 Evolution of Cloud Accounting

The evolution of cloud accounting can be traced through a series of transformative stages, each marked by technological advancements and changing business landscapes.

- *Early Adoption:* In the early 2000s, cloud accounting platforms emerged, providing basic functionalities like online invoicing and expense tracking. These solutions laid the groundwork for the more sophisticated systems we see today.

- *Integration with Business Processes:* As businesses sought more comprehensive solutions, cloud accounting platforms evolved to integrate with other business processes, such as inventory management, payroll, and customer relationship management (CRM).

- *Automation and AI Integration:* Recent developments have seen the integration of automation and artificial intelligence (AI) in cloud accounting, automating routine tasks, improving accuracy, and enabling data-driven insights for better decision-making.

2.3 Advantages and Challenges

Advantages:

- *Real-time Collaboration:* Cloud accounting facilitates real-time collaboration among accountants, clients, and other stakeholders. This enhances communication, reduces delays, and fosters a more dynamic working environment.

- *Accessibility and Mobility:* The ability to access financial data from anywhere with an internet connection provides unparalleled mobility. This is particularly beneficial for professionals who need to work remotely or collaborate across different locations.

- *Cost Savings:* Cloud accounting eliminates the need for significant upfront investments in hardware and software. The subscription-based model allows businesses to pay for the services they use, optimizing costs and resource allocation.

- *Scalability:* Cloud accounting platforms offer scalability, enabling businesses to easily adjust their computing resources based on changing needs. This flexibility ensures that the system can grow with the organization.

Challenges:

- *Security Concerns:* Storing financial data on remote servers raises security concerns. While cloud providers implement robust security measures, it is crucial for users to adopt best practices and ensure compliance with data protection regulations.

- *Internet Dependency:* Cloud accounting heavily relies on internet connectivity. Downtime or disruptions in internet service can hinder access to financial data and disrupt accounting processes.

- *Transition Challenges:* Transitioning from traditional accounting systems to cloud-based solutions can pose implementation challenges. Resistance to change, training requirements, and data migration complexities are common hurdles.

In navigating the complexities of cloud accounting, understanding these key concepts, the evolutionary journey, and the inherent advantages and challenges equips professionals to make informed decisions and harness the full potential of this transformative technology.

3

Current State of Accounting in India

The accounting profession in India is undergoing a metamorphosis, driven by a confluence of economic growth, technological advancements, and a dynamic regulatory environment. This report delves into the current state of accounting in India, highlighting key trends, challenges, and the exciting opportunities that lie ahead.

A Flourishing Industry:

India boasts a burgeoning accounting industry, ranking among the world's largest with over 3,50,000 Chartered Accountants and a similar number of cost and management accountants. This signifies the growing importance of professional financial services in the Indian economy. The demand for skilled accountants extends beyond traditional roles in public accounting firms. Businesses of all sizes, from burgeoning startups to established corporations, require financial expertise to navigate complex regulations, manage cash flow effectively, and make data-driven decisions. This has led to the emergence of a diverse accounting ecosystem encompassing:

- **Accounting firms:** These firms provide a comprehensive suite of services, including audit and assurance, tax advisory, corporate finance, and management consulting.

- **In-house accounting teams:** Many companies, particularly large corporations, have established in-house accounting teams to manage their day-to-day financial operations.

- **Freelance accountants and bookkeepers:** The rise of the gig economy has created a space for freelance accountants and bookkeepers who cater to the needs of startups, small businesses, and individuals.

Tech-Driven Transformation:

The accounting profession in India is witnessing a significant technological shift. Cloud-based accounting solutions are rapidly gaining traction in the Indian market. These solutions offer enhanced accessibility, cost-effectiveness, and robust security, streamlining financial management for businesses and fostering remote collaboration. Accounting firms are also increasingly leveraging automation and artificial intelligence (AI) tools. These technologies automate repetitive tasks like data entry and bookkeeping, allowing accountants to focus on:

- **Providing strategic advisory:** By analysing financial data and identifying trends, accountants can provide valuable insights to clients, helping them make informed business decisions and achieve their strategic goals.

- **Risk management:** Technology can be used to identify and mitigate financial risks, safeguarding a company's financial health.

- **Enhanced client service:** Automation frees up accountants' time to provide more personalized and responsive service to their clients.

Regulatory Landscape and Compliance:

The Indian government's emphasis on regulatory compliance has intensified with initiatives like the Goods and Services Tax (GST). This necessitates continuous learning and adaptation for accounting professionals to ensure their clients remain compliant. Additionally, Indian accounting standards (Ind AS) are undergoing a process of convergence with International Financial Reporting Standards (IFRS). This promotes global harmonization and transparency in financial reporting practices, enhancing investor confidence and facilitating international trade.

Challenges and the Road Ahead:

The rapid growth of the industry has created a growing demand for skilled accounting professionals with expertise in areas like:

- **Technology:** Understanding and leveraging accounting technology solutions is becoming increasingly important.

- **Compliance:** Staying abreast of the ever-evolving regulatory landscape is crucial for success.

- **Data analytics:** The ability to analyze financial data and extract meaningful insights is a valuable skill for accountants in the digital age.

Bridging this skills gap requires targeted training and education programs to ensure a continuous pipeline of qualified talent. The accounting industry is also witnessing increased competition, potentially leading to consolidation among firms. Adapting to new technologies, diversifying service offerings, and delivering value-added services will be key differentiators for success in this evolving environment.

The current state of accounting in India is characterized by dynamism and growth. The profession is actively embracing technology, adapting to changing regulations, and catering to the evolving needs of businesses. While challenges exist, the future of accounting in India appears bright, offering exciting opportunities for qualified professionals who can leverage technology, provide strategic guidance, and navigate the evolving regulatory landscape. By continuously developing their skillsets and embracing innovation, Indian accounting professionals are well-positioned to play a pivotal role in the country's economic growth story.

3.1 Traditional Accounting Practices

In India, traditional accounting practices have deep roots, shaped by a historical context that emphasizes meticulous record-keeping and adherence to established norms. Some prominent features include:

- *Manual Ledger Systems:* Many businesses in India still rely on manual ledger systems, where accountants meticulously record financial transactions in physical ledgers. This time-consuming process, while methodical, is prone to errors and lacks the efficiency demanded by today's dynamic business environment.

- *Paper-Based Processes:* The use of physical documents for invoicing, receipts, and financial reports remains prevalent. This not only contributes to a heavy reliance on physical storage but also complicates collaboration and accessibility.

- *Tax Compliance Challenges:* The intricate tax structure in India, including Goods and Services Tax (GST), places a significant burden on accountants. Navigating complex regulations manually can lead to errors, delays, and increased compliance risks.

3.2 Challenges Faced by Practicing Chartered Accountants

Practicing Chartered Accountants in India encounter a myriad of challenges, hindering their ability to deliver efficient and value-added services. Some notable challenges include:

- *High Compliance Burden:* The ever-changing regulatory landscape and intricate tax structures in India pose a substantial compliance burden on Chartered Accountants. Navigating through the complexities of GST, income tax, and other regulations demands a high level of expertise and consumes a significant amount of time.

- *Limited Access to Financial Data:* Traditional accounting practices often result in siloed information, making it challenging for Chartered Accountants to access real-time financial data. This limitation impedes their ability to provide timely insights and strategic advice to clients.

- *Client Expectations and Communication:* Clients increasingly expect more than just compliance services. They seek strategic guidance and proactive insights from their Chartered Accountants. Balancing these expectations with the constraints of traditional practices poses a communication challenge.

- *Time-Consuming Manual Processes:* Manual data entry and reconciliation processes are time-consuming and prone to errors. This hampers the efficiency of accounting operations and leaves little room for Chartered Accountants to focus on value-added tasks.

3.3 Need for Technological Integration

Recognizing the challenges faced by practicing Chartered Accountants in India, there is an urgent need for technological integration within the accounting profession. The adoption of modern technologies, particularly cloud accounting, can address these challenges and usher in a new era of efficiency and innovation. Key considerations include:

- *Real-time Collaboration:* Cloud accounting platforms facilitate real-time collaboration between Chartered

Accountants and their clients, enabling seamless communication, access to live financial data, and collaborative decision-making.

- *Automation of Routine Tasks:* Embracing technology allows for the automation of routine and time-consuming tasks, such as data entry and reconciliation. This automation not only enhances accuracy but also frees up valuable time for Chartered Accountants to focus on strategic advisory roles.

- *Enhanced Compliance:* Technological solutions can streamline compliance processes by providing real-time updates on regulatory changes, automating compliance checks, and ensuring accurate adherence to tax laws.

- *Client Relationship Management:* Cloud accounting platforms enable Chartered Accountants to move beyond transactional relationships with clients. By providing insights, analysis, and proactive advisory services, Chartered Accountants can strengthen their client relationships and become indispensable business partners.

In navigating the current state of accounting in India, the integration of technology emerges as a crucial pathway for Chartered Accountants to overcome challenges, enhance their services, and position themselves as strategic advisors in a rapidly evolving business landscape.

Key Features of Cloud Accounting

As we delve into the realm of cloud accounting, it becomes evident that its transformative power lies in a myriad of features that address the evolving needs of the modern accounting profession. In this chapter, we explore the key features that make cloud accounting a game-changer for practicing Chartered Accountants in India.

4.1 Real-time Collaboration

Real-time collaboration refers to the ability for multiple people to work on a project or task simultaneously, with everyone seeing the changes made by others instantly. It eliminates the need for waiting for someone to finish their part before you can begin yours, significantly increasing efficiency and communication.

Here are some key aspects of real-time collaboration:

- **Simultaneous work:** Everyone involved can edit, modify, or contribute to the project at the same time. This is a stark contrast to traditional methods where people take turns working on a document or project.

- **Instant updates:**

Changes made by one person are immediately visible to all collaborators. This eliminates confusion and ensures everyone is on the same page.

- **Improved communication:**

 Real-time collaboration fosters better communication as team members can discuss changes, ask questions, and provide feedback as they work.

- **Increased productivity:**

By eliminating the back-and-forth of traditional methods, real-time collaboration allows teams to work faster and complete projects more efficiently.

- **Enhanced engagement:**

The ability to see the project evolve in real-time keeps everyone engaged and motivated.

Benefits of Real-time Collaboration:

Faster project completion: Teams can complete projects in less time by working together simultaneously.

- **Improved accuracy:** Real-time updates minimize the risk of errors and inconsistencies.

- **Enhanced decision-making:** Instant access to information and feedback allows for better-informed decisions.

- **Boosted innovation:** Real-time brainstorming and idea sharing can spark creativity and innovation.

- **Greater team satisfaction:**

  Improved communication and a sense of shared accomplishment can lead to higher team morale.

Examples of Real-time Collaboration Tools:

- **Document editing software:** Google Docs, Microsoft 365, and Zoho Docs allow multiple users to edit documents simultaneously.

- **Project management tools:** Asana, Trello, and Monday.com enable teams to collaborate on tasks, share files, and track progress in real-time.

- **Video conferencing platforms:** Zoom, Microsoft Teams, and Google Meet allow for face-to-face communication and real-time collaboration on presentations or whiteboards.

- **Design tools:** Figma and Canva allow multiple designers to work on the same design project simultaneously.

Real-time collaboration has become an essential aspect of modern teamwork, especially for geographically dispersed teams or those working remotely. By leveraging these tools and fostering a collaborative work environment, businesses can unlock significant improvements in communication, efficiency, and overall project success.

4.2 Accessibility and Mobility

In the context of cloud accounting, accessibility and mobility translate to the ease with which users can access and manage their financial data. Cloud technology offers significant advantages in both accessibility and mobility, making it a powerful tool for businesses of all sizes.

Accessibility:

- **Remote access:** Cloud accounting allows users to access their financial data from anywhere with an internet connection. This eliminates the need to be physically present in an office or have the software installed on a specific computer. It's ideal for remote workforces, geographically dispersed teams, and business owners on the go.

- **Device Agnostic:** Cloud accounting software is accessible from various devices, including laptops, tablets, and smartphones. This provides flexibility and convenience, allowing users to manage their finances on the move or from any location with an internet connection.

- **Simplified User Interface:** Cloud accounting software is designed to be user-friendly, even for those without extensive accounting knowledge. Intuitive interfaces and helpful tutorials make it easy for anyone to access and manage their financial data.

Mobility:

- **Real-time updates:** Cloud accounting provides real-time access to financial data. Users can view transactions, generate reports, and monitor cash flow instantly, regardless of their location. This mobility empowers informed decision-making based on the latest financial information.

- **Collaboration:** Cloud accounting facilitates collaboration between accountants, bookkeepers, and business owners. Everyone can access the same financial data simultaneously, fostering transparency and streamlining communication. This collaborative environment allows for efficient teamwork, even for geographically dispersed teams.

- **Integration with mobile apps:** Many cloud accounting solutions offer mobile apps that allow users to view key financial information, approve payments, and perform basic accounting tasks on their smartphones or tablets. This enhances mobility further, allowing users to manage their finances from anywhere, anytime.

Benefits of Accessibility and Mobility in Cloud Accounting:

- **Improved Efficiency:** Easy access to financial data allows for faster decision-making and streamlined financial management processes.

- **Enhanced Collaboration:** Real-time updates and collaboration tools promote better communication and teamwork.

- **Increased Productivity:** Mobility allows users to manage finances on the go, maximizing productivity and minimizing time spent in the office.

- **Reduced Costs:** Eliminates the need for expensive software licenses and on-premise IT infrastructure.

- **Improved Business Continuity:** Cloud-based data storage ensures accessibility even in case of hardware failure or natural disasters.

Overall, accessibility and mobility are key features that make cloud accounting a compelling solution for businesses today. By enabling remote access, real-time updates, and seamless collaboration, cloud accounting empowers businesses to manage their finances efficiently, adapt to changing circumstances, and thrive in the digital age.

4.3 Security Measures

Cloud accounting offers numerous benefits, but security is a paramount concern for businesses entrusting their financial data to a remote server. Here's a breakdown of some key security measures employed by cloud accounting providers to safeguard your data:

Data Encryption:

- **At Rest:** Data is encrypted while stored on the cloud provider's servers. This encryption scrambles your data, making it unreadable even if someone were to gain unauthorized access to the server.

- **In Transit:** Data is encrypted while being transferred between your device and the cloud server. This ensures that even if someone intercepts the data transmission, they won't be able to decipher it.

Access Controls:

- **Multi-Factor Authentication (MFA):** This extra layer of security requires more than just a username and password to log in. It might involve a code sent to your phone or a fingerprint scan, making unauthorized access significantly more difficult.

- **User Permissions:** Cloud accounting software allows you to set permissions for different users, restricting access to sensitive data based on their roles and responsibilities.

Data Backup and Disaster Recovery:

- **Regular Backups:** Cloud providers regularly back up your data to ensure its recovery in case of server failure or accidental data loss.

- **Disaster Recovery Plans:** Cloud providers have robust disaster recovery plans in place to ensure business continuity in Case of natural disasters or other unforeseen events. These plans ensure your data remains accessible and secure even in the event of disruptions.

Compliance and Security Audits:

- **Industry Standards:** Reputable cloud accounting providers comply with industry-recognized security standards like SOC 2, ensuring they have robust security controls in place.

- **Regular Audits:** Cloud providers undergo regular security audits by independent third parties to verify their compliance with security standards and identify any potential vulnerabilities.

Security Best Practices:

- **Strong Passwords:** Enforce the use of strong passwords and encourage regular password changes to minimize the risk of unauthorized access.

- **Software Updates:** Keep your cloud accounting software and devices updated with the latest security patches to address any known vulnerabilities.

- **Be Wary of Phishing Attacks:** Educate your employees about phishing scams and how to identify suspicious emails or links that could compromise their login credentials.

Choosing a Secure Cloud Accounting Provider:

- **Research Security Features:** When choosing a cloud accounting provider, investigate their security measures, compliance certifications, and data privacy practices.

- **Understand Your Needs:** Choose a provider that offers security features that meet your specific business needs and data sensitivity requirements.

- **Read Reviews and Ask Questions:** Read reviews from other users and don't hesitate to ask the provider about their security protocols and data protection measures.

Cloud accounting providers take data security very seriously. By employing robust encryption, access controls, data backup, and disaster recovery plans, they strive to safeguard your financial information. However, it's crucial for businesses to adopt best practices, choose a reputable provider, and remain informed about potential security threats.

4.4 Integration with Other Business Tools

Cloud accounting offers a plethora of benefits, but its true power lies in its ability to seamlessly integrate with other business tools. This integration fosters an interconnected ecosystem, streamlining workflows, eliminating manual data entry, and boosting overall efficiency. Let's delve into the world of cloud accounting integrations and explore the advantages they offer:

Benefits of Cloud Accounting Integration:

- **Reduced Errors and Improved Accuracy:** Eliminating manual data entry between different software programs minimizes the risk of errors and inconsistencies. This ensures data integrity across your entire business ecosystem.

- **Streamlined Workflows:** Integration automates data exchange between applications, saving time and effort. Say goodbye to repetitive tasks and hello to a smoother, more efficient workflow.

- **Enhanced Collaboration:** Integrations enable data sharing and collaboration across different departments. Accounting, sales, marketing, and inventory teams can all work from the same set of data, promoting better communication and decision-making.

- **Real-time Insights:** Integrated applications provide real-time access to consolidated data from various sources. This empowers you to make informed decisions based on a holistic view of your business operations.

- **Increased Productivity:** By automating tasks and streamlining workflows, integrations free up valuable time for your team to focus on higher-level tasks and strategic initiatives.

Popular Cloud Accounting Integrations:

- **CRM (Customer Relationship Management):** Integrate your cloud accounting software with your CRM to synchronize customer data, track invoices and payments, and gain valuable insights into customer behavior and spending habits.

- **Ecommerce Platforms:** Seamless integration allows for automatic order processing, inventory management, and revenue recognition. This ensures your accounting data reflects your online sales accurately.

- **Payroll Systems:** Simplify payroll processing by integrating your accounting software with your payroll system. This automates data transfer for salaries, taxes, and deductions, minimizing errors and saving time.

- **Inventory Management Software:** Integrate your accounting software with inventory management software to track stock levels, automate purchase orders, and maintain accurate cost of goods sold (COGS) calculations.

- **Project Management Tools:** Track project expenses, generate invoices for billable hours, and analyze project profitability by integrating accounting software with project management tools.

- **Business Intelligence (BI) Tools:** Integrate your accounting data with BI tools for powerful data analysis and reporting. Gain insights into financial trends, identify areas for improvement, and make data-driven business decisions.

Choosing the Right Integrations:

The specific integrations your business needs will depend on your industry, size, and unique workflows. Here are some factors to consider:

- **Identify Your Needs:** Are you looking to streamline invoicing, automate expense tracking, or gain deeper customer insights? Analyze your business processes to identify pain points that integrations can address.

- **Evaluate Existing Tools:** Consider the business tools you already use and choose cloud accounting software that integrates seamlessly with them.

- **Scalability:** Select a cloud accounting solution that can grow with your business and offers integrations with additional tools as your needs evolve.

Cloud accounting integration unlocks a world of possibilities. By connecting your financial data with other business tools, you can create a unified ecosystem that empowers efficient operations, insightful decision-making, and a data-driven approach to business growth. Explore the world of integrations, identify the ones that best suit your needs, and watch your business soar to new heights.

4.5 Cost Savings

Cloud accounting has revolutionized the way businesses manage their finances. Beyond the benefits of accessibility, collaboration, and powerful features, cloud accounting offers significant cost savings for businesses of all sizes. Here's how:

Reduced Upfront Costs:

- **No Software Licenses:** Cloud accounting eliminates the need for expensive software licenses that require upfront investments. You typically pay a monthly subscription fee based on your usage, making it a budget-friendly option for startups and small businesses.

- **No Hardware Costs:** There's no need to purchase expensive servers or workstations to run accounting software. Cloud providers handle the infrastructure, eliminating the associated hardware costs and maintenance expenses.

Improved Operational Efficiency:

- **Reduced IT Costs:** Cloud accounting minimizes the need for dedicated IT staff for software installation, maintenance, and updates. Cloud providers handle these tasks, freeing up your IT resources for other critical projects.

- **Automated Workflows:**

  Cloud accounting automates many manual tasks like data entry, invoice processing, and bank reconciliations. This saves time and reduces the risk of errors, leading to increased efficiency and reduced labor costs.

- **Improved Collaboration:**

  Real-time data access and collaboration features eliminate the need for email exchanges and manual data transfers between accountants, bookkeepers, and business owners. This streamlines communication and reduces administrative overhead.

Scalability and Flexibility:

- **Pay-as-you-go Model:** Cloud accounting typically follows a subscription model with tiered plans. You only pay for the features and user access you need, allowing you to scale your plan as your business grows. This eliminates the need to invest in expensive software upgrades as your accounting needs evolve.

- **Reduced Paperwork:** Cloud accounting encourages a paperless environment, saving costs on paper, printing, storage, and document retrieval.

Additional Cost-Saving Benefits:

- **Enhanced Compliance:** Automatic updates ensure you're always using the latest tax regulations and accounting standards, minimizing the risk of penalties and associated costs.

- **Improved Cash Flow Management:** Real-time insights into your finances empower you to make informed decisions about spending, invoicing, and cash flow management, potentially leading to cost reductions and improved financial health.

- **Reduced Risk of Data Loss:** Cloud providers offer robust security measures and data backup solutions, minimizing the risk of data loss and the associated recovery costs.

Cloud Accounting vs Traditional Software:

Traditional accounting software often involves:

- High upfront costs for licenses and hardware

- Ongoing maintenance and update expenses

- Limited accessibility and collaboration features

- Difficulty in scaling with business growth

Cloud accounting, on the other hand, offers a cost-effective and scalable solution that eliminates these pain points.

Cloud accounting offers a compelling value proposition for businesses seeking to reduce costs and improve financial management. From eliminating upfront investments to streamlining workflows and enhancing efficiency, cloud accounting empowers businesses to focus on their core operations while keeping their finances in order.

5

Popular Cloud Accounting Platforms

In the ever-expanding landscape of cloud accounting, several platforms have risen to prominence, offering diverse features and functionalities tailored to the needs of businesses and Chartered Accountants in India. In this chapter, we explore some of the popular cloud accounting platforms, highlighting their key attributes and considering factors for comparison.

5.1 QuickBooks Online

QuickBooks Online (QBO) is a widely recognized and powerful cloud accounting platform designed to cater to businesses of all sizes. Its popularity stems from its comprehensive feature set, user-friendly interface, and strong integrations with other business tools. Here's a closer look at what QuickBooks Online offers:

Strengths of QuickBooks Online:

- ***Feature Rich:*** *QBO boasts a robust suite of features encompassing core accounting functionalities like* *invoicing, expense tracking, bill payment, and bank reconciliation. It also offers advanced features for inventory management, project tracking, and financial reporting. This makes it a versatile solution that can be adapted to meet the growing needs of a business. For instance, a small business owner can start with basic invoicing and expense tracking, then easily add on features like inventory management or project tracking as their business scales and their accounting requirements become more complex.*

- ***Scalability:*** *QBO is designed to scale with your business. It offers various subscription plans with increasing features and user capacities, allowing you to adapt the platform to your evolving needs. This eliminates the need to constantly switch accounting software as your business grows, potentially saving time and resources in the long run.*

- ***Ease of Use:*** *While offering a rich feature set, QBO maintains a user-friendly interface. Even users without extensive accounting experience can navigate the platform effectively, with helpful tutorials and guides available. An intuitive* *dashboard provides a clear overview of your financial health, with easy access to key metrics and reports.*

- ***Strong Integrations:*** *QBO integrates seamlessly with a vast ecosystem of popular business applications, including CRM platforms, inventory management systems, and payment processors. This streamlines workflows and eliminates the need for manual data entry across different software programs. For example, you can integrate QBO with your CRM to automatically sync customer data and invoices, saving time and reducing the risk of errors.*

- ***Mobility:*** *QBO offers a mobile app that allows you to access your financial data, manage invoices, and approve payments on the go. This mobility empowers informed decision-making and facilitates remote work. You can review financial reports, approve bills, or send invoices to clients from your smartphone or tablet, ensuring you stay on top of your finances even when you're away from the office.*

Considerations for Using QuickBooks Online:

- **Cost:** *While QBO offers a free trial, its subscription plans can be more expensive compared to some competitors, especially for basic accounting needs. For businesses with straightforward accounting requirements, there might be more cost-effective options available.*

- **Complexity:** *The extensive feature set might be overwhelming for very small businesses or those with straightforward accounting requirements. If you're a sole proprietor with a limited number of clients and transactions, exploring a more basic accounting solution might be sufficient.*

- **Customization:** *QBO offers some customization options, but its functionalities are not as customizable as some accounting software designed for larger enterprises. Businesses with highly specific accounting needs or complex industry regulations might require a more customizable accounting solution.*

Who Should Use QuickBooks Online:

QBO is a great choice for:

- ***Small and Medium Businesses (SMBs):*** *Its scalability and feature range make it suitable for businesses growing beyond the basic accounting needs often addressed by entry-level solutions. As a business scales, QBO can grow with it, accommodating increasingly complex accounting requirements.*

- ***Freelancers with Complex Needs:*** *If you're a freelancer with multiple clients, projects, or inventory management requirements, QBO's features can streamline your financial operations. QBO can help you manage client invoices, track project expenses, and gain valuable insights into your business profitability.*

- ***Businesses that Need Strong Integrations:*** *QBO's vast integration network makes it ideal for businesses that rely on various tools to manage different aspects of their operations. By integrating QBO with your existing business applications, you* *can create a unified ecosystem that enhances efficiency and data accuracy.*

QuickBooks Online is a powerful and feature-rich cloud accounting platform that caters to a wide range of businesses. Its user-friendly interface, scalability, and robust integrations make it a popular choice for businesses seeking a comprehensive accounting solution. However, its cost structure and feature complexity might be a consideration for very small businesses or those with basic accounting needs. Carefully evaluate your business requirements and budget to determine if QBO is the ideal fit for your financial management needs.

5.2 Xero

Xero is a leading cloud accounting platform designed specifically with small and medium-sized businesses (SMBs) in mind. It boasts a user-friendly interface, robust features for core accounting tasks, and seamless integrations with various business tools. Here's a detailed breakdown of what Xero offers:

Strengths of Xero:

- ***Simplicity and Ease of Use:*** *Xero prioritizes user-friendliness. Its clean and intuitive interface makes it easy to navigate for business owners and non-accountants alike. Even those without extensive accounting experience can quickly learn the ropes and manage their finances effectively. The platform provides clear instructions, helpful tutorials, and a well-organized dashboard that simplifies financial management.*

- ***Focus on Core Accounting Functions:*** *Xero excels in core accounting functionalities like invoicing, expense tracking, bill payments, and bank reconciliation. It automates many repetitive tasks, saving time and minimizing errors. Features like online invoicing with customizable templates, automatic expense categorization, and real-time bank feeds streamline the accounting process for busy business owners.*

- ***Inventory Management:*** *Xero offers robust inventory management capabilities, allowing you to track stock levels, generate purchase orders, and* *manage inventory costs. This is particularly beneficial for businesses that sell products and need to maintain accurate inventory records.*

- ***Collaboration Features:*** *Xero facilitates collaboration between business owners, accountants, and bookkeepers. Multiple users can access the platform simultaneously, share data securely, and work together seamlessly. This fosters transparency and streamlines communication regarding financial matters.*

- ***Integration Ecosystem:*** *Xero integrates with a wide range of business applications, including CRM platforms, payment processors, and point-of-sale (POS) systems. This integration capability eliminates the need for manual data entry across different software programs and empowers a more efficient workflow.*

- ***Mobility:*** *Xero offers a mobile app that allows you to manage your finances on the go. You can access financial reports, approve bills, send invoices, and capture receipts from your smartphone or tablet,* *ensuring you stay in control of your finances even when you're away from the office.*

Considerations for Using Xero:

- ***Cost:*** *While Xero offers a free trial, its subscription plans can be more expensive compared to some basic accounting solutions. For businesses with very limited accounting needs and a low transaction volume, there might be more cost-effective options available.*

- ***Limited Customization:*** *Xero offers some customization options, but its functionalities are not as customizable as some accounting software designed for larger enterprises with complex accounting requirements. However, for most SMBs, the level of customization offered by Xero is sufficient.*

- ***Advanced Features:*** *While Xero excels in core accounting functionalities, it might lack some advanced features needed by larger businesses or those in specific industries with highly specialized accounting needs. For instance, businesses requiring* *advanced inventory management features or payroll processing might need to explore alternative platforms.*

Who Should Use Xero:

Small and Medium Businesses: *Xero is a perfect fit for SMBs looking for a user-friendly and comprehensive accounting solution. Its focus on core accounting tasks, inventory management capabilities, and collaboration features cater to the needs of growing businesses.*

Freelancers and Sole Proprietors: *Xero can be a good option for freelancers and sole proprietors who need to manage invoices, track expenses, and gain insights into their business performance. The user-friendly interface makes it easy to learn and use, even for those without extensive accounting knowledge.*

Businesses Seeking Strong Integrations: *If your business relies on various tools and applications, Xero's strong integration capabilities can be a major advantage. By integrating Xero with* *your existing business ecosystem, you can create a unified workflow and eliminate data silos.*

Xero is a popular cloud accounting platform that empowers small and medium businesses with user-friendly tools to manage their finances effectively. Its focus on core accounting functionalities, collaboration features, and strong integrations make it a compelling choice for businesses seeking a streamlined and efficient accounting solution. However, consider your business size, budget, and specific accounting needs to determine if Xero is the ideal fit for your financial management requirements.

5.3 Zoho Books

Zoho Books is a comprehensive cloud accounting platform offered by Zoho, a leading provider of business software solutions. It caters to businesses of all sizes, from startups to established enterprises, offering a scalable solution that can grow with your needs. Here's a closer look at the key features and benefits of Zoho Books:

Strengths of Zoho Books:

- ***Scalability and Customization:*** *Zoho Books is designed to scale with your business. It offers a variety of subscription plans with increasing features and user capacities. Additionally, Zoho Books provides a high level of customization compared to other cloud accounting platforms. You can tailor the platform to your specific accounting needs by creating custom fields, workflows, and reports. This makes it suitable for businesses with unique accounting requirements or those in niche industries.*

- ***Inventory Management:*** *Zoho Books offers robust inventory management features, including product categorization, barcode scanning, purchase order management, and low-stock alerts. This empowers businesses to maintain accurate inventory levels, optimize stock control, and streamline their sales processes.*

- ***Project Management:*** *Zoho Books integrates seamlessly with other Zoho applications, including Zoho Projects. This integration allows you to track* *project expenses, generate invoices for billable hours, and analyze project profitability directly within Zoho Books. This streamlines project costing and financial management for businesses that rely on project-based work.*

- ***Automation Features:*** *Zoho Books automates many repetitive tasks, such as recurring invoices, bank reconciliation, and expense categorization. This saves time, minimizes errors, and allows you to focus on more strategic financial activities.*

- ***Multilingual and Multicurrency Support:*** *Zoho Books caters to businesses operating internationally. It supports multiple languages and currencies, allowing you to manage finances, generate invoices, and track transactions seamlessly across different locations and currencies.*

- ***Integration Ecosystem:*** *Zoho Books integrates with a wide range of popular business applications, including CRM platforms, payment processors, and e-commerce platforms. This integration capability fosters a unified business ecosystem and eliminates* *the need for manual data entry across different software programs.*

Considerations for Using Zoho Books:

- ***Learning Curve:*** *While Zoho Books offers a user-friendly interface, its extensive feature set might require a slightly steeper learning curve compared to some basic accounting solutions. However, Zoho provides comprehensive training materials and support resources to help users get acquainted with the platform.*

- ***Cost:*** *Zoho Books offers a free plan with limited features. Paid subscription plans can be more expensive than some basic accounting solutions, particularly for businesses with straightforward accounting needs. Carefully evaluate your needs and budget before choosing a plan.*

- ***Target Audience:*** *Zoho Books might be an overkill for very small businesses or freelancers with basic accounting requirements. However, for growing businesses, startups, and established enterprises with complex accounting needs or those operating* *internationally, Zoho Books offers a powerful and scalable solution.*

Who Should Use Zoho Books:

- ***Growing Businesses:*** *Zoho Books' scalability and customization features make it ideal for businesses that are experiencing growth and require a solution that can adapt to their evolving accounting needs.*

- ***Businesses with Project-Based Work:*** *If your business relies on projects, Zoho Books' integration with Zoho Projects simplifies project costing and financial management, providing valuable insights into project profitability.*

- ***International Businesses:*** *Zoho Books' multilingual and multicurrency support caters to businesses operating internationally, allowing them to manage finances and generate invoices seamlessly across different locations and currencies.*

- ***Businesses Seeking Advanced Features:*** *Zoho Books caters to businesses that require advanced features beyond basic accounting functionalities. Inventory management, project tracking, and the* *ability to create highly customized workflows make Zoho Books a powerful accounting solution.*

Zoho Books is a feature-rich and scalable cloud accounting platform that empowers businesses of all sizes to manage their finances effectively. Its robust functionalities, customization options, and integration capabilities make it a strong contender for businesses seeking a comprehensive accounting solution that can grow with them. However, consider your business size, budget, and specific accounting needs to determine if Zoho Books is the ideal fit for your financial management requirements.

5.4 Tally on Cloud

Tally is a popular accounting software widely used in India and some other regions. Tally on Cloud allows you to access and use this software through a cloud platform, offering potential benefits and considerations for businesses:

Advantages of Tally on Cloud:

- ***Accessibility:*** *Access your Tally data from anywhere, anytime, using a web browser or mobile* app. This eliminates the need to be physically present in the office to work on your accounts.

- **Remote Collaboration:** Multiple users can access and work on Tally data simultaneously, fostering collaboration between accountants, bookkeepers, and business owners.

- **Scalability:** Cloud-based solutions typically offer easy scaling of resources. As your business grows and your accounting needs increase, you can easily upgrade your cloud plan to accommodate additional users or data storage.

- **Disaster Recovery:** Cloud providers offer robust data backup and disaster recovery solutions. In case of hardware failure or natural disasters, your Tally data remains secure and accessible.

- **Reduced Costs:** Eliminate the upfront costs of purchasing server hardware and software licenses. You typically pay a monthly subscription fee for Tally on Cloud, potentially reducing IT infrastructure expenses.

- ***Automatic Updates:*** *Cloud providers handle software updates and maintenance, ensuring you're always using the latest version of Tally and eliminating the need for manual updates.*

- ***Improved Security:*** *Cloud providers invest heavily in security measures to protect your data. This can be especially beneficial for businesses that might not have the resources to implement robust security measures on-premise.*

Considerations for Tally on Cloud:

- ***Internet Reliance:*** *Continuous internet connectivity is essential for accessing Tally on Cloud. Any internet outages could disrupt your ability to work on your accounts.*

- ***Data Security:*** *While cloud providers offer security measures, it's crucial to choose a reputable provider with a strong track record of data security. Carefully evaluate their security practices and ensure your data is encrypted both at rest and in transit.*

- ***Vendor Lock-in:*** *Switching from one cloud provider to another might be complex, especially if your data* *is heavily customized within the Tally environment. Carefully evaluate your needs and choose a provider with a good reputation and long-term commitment to the Tally platform.*

- ***Integration Limitations:*** *Tally on Cloud might not integrate seamlessly with all third-party applications compared to some cloud-native accounting platforms. Research integration capabilities to ensure compatibility with your existing business tools.*

Is Tally on Cloud Right for You?

Tally on Cloud can be a suitable option for businesses that:

- *Already use Tally and want to leverage the benefits of cloud computing.*

- *Require remote access to their accounting data.*

- *Have concerns about data security and disaster recovery.*

- *Need a scalable solution to accommodate business growth.*

However, carefully consider your internet connectivity, data security needs, and existing software integrations before migrating to Tally on Cloud.

Alternatives to Tally on Cloud:

If you're not tied to Tally or open to exploring other options, there are numerous cloud-native accounting platforms available, such as QuickBooks Online, Xero, and Zoho Books. These platforms offer similar functionalities as Tally on Cloud, potentially with a wider range of integrations and features tailored for a cloud-based environment.

Ultimately, the decision of whether to use Tally on Cloud or explore alternative cloud accounting solutions depends on your specific business needs and preferences. Carefully weigh the advantages and considerations to determine the best fit for your financial management requirements.

5.5 Comparisons and Considerations

When choosing a cloud accounting platform, it's essential to consider various factors, including the specific needs of the business, ease of use, pricing, and scalability. Some key considerations for comparison include:

- *User Interface:* Evaluate the user interface to ensure it aligns with the proficiency and preferences of the accounting team.

- *Features and Functionalities:* Compare the features offered by each platform, considering the specific accounting needs and industry requirements of the business.

- *Integration Capabilities:* Assess the integration capabilities of each platform, ensuring compatibility with other essential business tools.

- *Scalability:* Consider the scalability of the platform to accommodate the growing needs of the business over time.

- *Cost:* Compare the pricing structures of different platforms, including subscription fees, add-on costs, and any hidden charges.

By carefully considering these factors and exploring the features of popular cloud accounting platforms, Chartered Accountants in India can make informed decisions to enhance their practices and deliver value-added services to their clients.

6

Implementing Cloud Accounting in Practice

Embracing cloud accounting represents a significant shift in the way Chartered Accountants operate and deliver services. Successful implementation requires careful planning, addressing resistance, and investing in training. In this chapter, we explore the crucial steps to transition, strategies for overcoming resistance, and the importance of training and skill development.

6.1 Steps to Transition

Transitioning to cloud accounting can streamline your financial processes, boost accessibility, and enhance collaboration. Here's a roadmap to guide you through a smooth implementation:

1. Evaluation and Planning:

- **Assess Your Needs:** Identify your current accounting practices, pain points, and desired outcomes. What functionalities are crucial for your business? Consider factors like business size, transaction volume, and industry-specific requirements.

- **Research Cloud Accounting Options:** Explore popular cloud accounting platforms like QuickBooks Online, Xero, and Zoho Books. Evaluate features, pricing plans, integrations with your existing business tools, and ease of use.

- **Develop an Implementation Plan:** Outline the steps involved in the transition, including data migration, user training, and go-live date. Assign roles and responsibilities to ensure a smooth rollout.

2. Data Migration and System Setup:

- **Choose a Data Migration Strategy:** Work with your chosen cloud accounting provider to determine the best approach for transferring your historical financial data. This might involve exporting data from your existing software or working with the provider's migration tools.

- **Cleanse and Organize Data:** Before migration, ensure your existing accounting data is accurate and organized. This minimizes errors and streamlines the import process.

- **Set Up the Cloud Accounting Platform:**

  Configure the platform according to your business needs. This might involve setting up your chart of accounts, defining tax rates, and customizing invoice templates.

3. User Training and Communication:

- **Train Your Team:**

  Provide comprehensive training to your accounting staff, bookkeepers, and anyone who will use the new system. Training should cover basic functionalities, advanced features, and best practices for cloud accounting.

- **Address Concerns and Encourage Adoption:**

  Clearly communicate the benefits of cloud accounting to your team and address any concerns or resistance to change. Encourage them to explore the new features and provide feedback.

4. Go-Live and Ongoing Support:

- **Launch the Cloud Accounting System:** Set a go-live date and ensure all data is migrated, users are trained, and any technical glitches are resolved.

- **Monitor and Refine:** Continuously monitor your cloud accounting system for any issues or areas for improvement. Regularly review user feedback and make adjustments to optimize efficiency.

- **Ongoing Support:** Leverage the support resources offered by your cloud accounting provider. They can answer questions, troubleshoot problems, and keep you updated on new features and functionalities.

Additional Tips for a Successful Transition:

- **Start with a Trial:** Many cloud accounting platforms offer free trials. Utilize this opportunity to test features, assess user experience, and ensure compatibility with your needs before committing to a paid plan.

- **Seek Professional Help:** Consider consulting with a cloud accounting specialist or your accountant.

They can guide you through the selection process, assist with data migration, and ensure a smooth transition.

- **Maintain Data Security:** Implement strong password policies, enable two-factor authentication, and regularly back up your data. Choose a cloud accounting provider with robust security measures to safeguard your financial information.

By following these steps and considering the additional tips, you can navigate the transition to cloud accounting seamlessly and unlock the numerous benefits it offers for your business. Remember, effective planning, clear communication, and ongoing support are key to a successful implementation.

6.2 Overcoming Resistance and Challenges

Resistance to change is a common hurdle in adopting new technologies, and cloud accounting is no exception. Addressing this resistance involves a combination of communication, collaboration, and showcasing the tangible benefits of the transition. Strategies include:

- *Communication and Education:* Clearly communicate the reasons for transitioning to cloud accounting, emphasizing the advantages for both the practice and its clients. Provide educational materials and demonstrations to showcasing the ease of use and benefits.

- *Involving Key Stakeholders:* Involve key stakeholders, including partners, managers, and staff, in the decision-making process. Encourage open dialogue to address concerns and gather insights that can inform the implementation strategy.

- *Highlighting Benefits:* Emphasize the specific benefits of cloud accounting, such as real-time collaboration, improved efficiency, and enhanced client services. Illustrate how these benefits align with the long-term goals and success of the practice.

- *Pilot Programs:* Consider implementing pilot programs with a select group of clients to demonstrate the advantages of cloud accounting in a controlled environment. Positive experiences from these pilot programs can help build confidence and enthusiasm.

6.3 Training and Skill Development

The successful implementation of cloud accounting hinges on the proficiency of the accounting team. Training and skill development are integral to ensuring that team members can effectively utilize the new technology. Key considerations include:

- *Comprehensive Training Programs:* Develop comprehensive training programs that cover the features and functionalities of the chosen cloud accounting platform. Include hands-on exercises and simulations to reinforce learning.

- *Continuous Learning Opportunities:* Cloud accounting platforms often receive updates and new features. Establish a culture of continuous learning, providing ongoing training opportunities to keep the team abreast of the latest advancements.

- *Certifications and Qualifications:* Encourage team members to pursue relevant certifications and qualifications related to cloud accounting.

Recognized certifications can validate their expertise and enhance their credibility in the industry.

- *Cross-functional Collaboration:* Foster collaboration between accounting and IT teams to ensure a holistic understanding of the technology infrastructure supporting cloud accounting. This collaboration enhances problem-solving capabilities and promotes a culture of innovation.

By meticulously following these steps, addressing resistance, and prioritizing training and skill development, Chartered Accountants can successfully implement cloud accounting in their practices, unlocking the full potential of technology to drive efficiency and deliver value to clients.

7

Benefits for Practicing Chartered Accountants

The adoption of cloud accounting in the Indian accounting landscape presents a multitude of advantages for practicing Chartered Accountants. From efficiency gains to fostering client relationships, cloud accounting serves as a catalyst for positive transformation. In this chapter, we delve into the key benefits that practicing Chartered Accountants can derive from embracing cloud accounting.

7.1 Improved Efficiency and Productivity

Cloud accounting revolutionizes the way Chartered Accountants manage and process financial data, leading to a substantial boost in efficiency and productivity. Key aspects include:

Streamlined workflows and automation:

- Cloud accounting automates many repetitive tasks such as data entry, bank reconciliation, and report generation. This frees up accountants from manual labor, allowing them to focus on more strategic financial analysis and planning. They can delve deeper into financial data to identify trends, assess financial health, and make data-driven recommendations to improve client profitability or optimize business operations.

- Automated workflows eliminate the need for manual data transfer between different software programs, reducing the risk of errors and inconsistencies. This improves data integrity and saves time previously spent on troubleshooting and correcting errors.

Real-time access and collaboration:

- Cloud-based accounting platforms allow you to access financial data from anywhere, anytime, with an internet connection. This eliminates the need to be physically present in the office to work on the accounts, fostering a more flexible work environment. This can be particularly beneficial for businesses with remote teams or those that require accountants to travel frequently.

- Real-time collaboration features enable accountants, bookkeepers, and business owners to work on the same data simultaneously, fostering better communication and faster decision-making. Imagine a scenario where a sales team closes a deal and can immediately update the accounting system, allowing the finance team to see the impact on cash flow and update financial forecasts in real-time. This level of collaboration can significantly improve the responsiveness and agility of a business.

Improved accessibility and mobility:

- Cloud accounting allows remote work flexibility, as you can access financial data from mobile devices using apps. This is beneficial for geographically dispersed teams or those who prefer a flexible work schedule. But the advantages extend beyond just work-life balance. Mobile access allows accountants to be more responsive to client inquiries and address urgent matters on the go, improving client satisfaction.

Increased accuracy and reduced errors:

- Data integration with various business tools eliminates the need for manual data entry across different software programs. This minimizes the risk of errors and ensures data accuracy across the financial ecosystem. Standardized data formats and automated workflows further enhance data integrity and reduce the likelihood of inconsistencies.

- Automatic software updates ensure accountants always have access to the latest features, tax regulations, and accounting standards, minimizing errors due to outdated software. This is particularly important for accountants who need to comply with complex or frequently changing regulations.

Overall impact on efficiency and productivity:

- By automating tasks, streamlining workflows, and improving accessibility, cloud accounting allows accounting teams to accomplish more in less time. This translates to cost savings as well, as businesses can reduce their reliance on overtime or additional staff to handle accounting tasks.

- Accountants can dedicate more time to value-added activities such as financial analysis, tax planning, and strategic consulting for clients. They can use their financial expertise to help clients make better business decisions, identify growth opportunities, and improve their overall financial health.

- Businesses gain improved financial visibility and control through real-time data and insights, enabling better decision-making and resource allocation. With a clear understanding of their financial performance, businesses can identify areas for improvement, optimize spending, and make data-driven decisions to achieve their strategic objectives.

Here are some additional points to consider:

- Cloud accounting platforms often offer a user-friendly interface, with features that simplify data entry and analysis, further enhancing efficiency. Intuitive dashboards and data visualization tools can empower even non-accountants to glean valuable insights from financial data.

- Scalable subscription plans allow businesses to choose a solution that meets their needs and grows with them, eliminating the need for expensive upfront software investments. This makes cloud accounting an accessible option for businesses of all sizes, from startups to established enterprises.

If you're looking to improve the efficiency and productivity of your accounting processes, cloud accounting is a powerful tool to consider. It can not only streamline workflows and reduce errors but also empower accountants to provide more strategic value to their clients and businesses to make data-driven decisions for long-term success.

7.2 Enhanced Client Relationships

Cloud accounting opens new avenues for Chartered Accountants to build stronger, more collaborative relationships with their clients. Key benefits include:

Improved Communication and Collaboration:

- **Real-time access:** Cloud accounting provides both Chartered Accountants and clients with real-time access to the same financial data. This eliminates information silos and fosters transparency. Clients can stay informed about their financial health, and Chartered Accountants can address client inquiries promptly with the most up-to-date information.

- **Efficient information sharing:** Secure client portals within cloud platforms allow for easy and secure sharing of financial documents, reports, and other relevant information. This streamlines communication and eliminates the need for time-consuming email exchanges or physical document delivery.

Proactive Financial Guidance:

- **Real-time insights:**

Cloud accounting offers real-time financial data and analytics, empowering Chartered Accountants to identify potential issues or opportunities early on. This enables them to provide proactive financial advice and guidance to clients, helping them avoid problems and make informed business decisions.

- **Strategic financial partnering:**

By leveraging cloud-based data and insights, Chartered Accountants can move beyond basic accounting tasks and act as strategic financial partners for their clients. They can collaborate with clients to develop financial plans, set budgets, and achieve long-term financial goals.

Increased Client Satisfaction:

- **Improved efficiency:** Cloud accounting automates tasks and streamlines workflows, saving both Chartered Accountants and clients valuable time. This allows Chartered Accountants to focus on higher-value activities such as financial analysis and client consultations.

- **Enhanced communication:** Real-time access, secure collaboration tools, and proactive communication fostered by cloud accounting lead to a more positive client experience. Clients feel informed, valued, and confident in their Chartered Accountant's ability to manage their finances effectively.

Additional benefits for client relationships:

- **Secure client portals:** Cloud platforms offer secure client portals where clients can access their financial information anytime, anywhere. This fosters trust and transparency in the client relationship.

- **Reduced paperwork:** Cloud accounting promotes a paperless environment, eliminating the need for physical document exchange and simplifying document management for both parties.

- **Improved accessibility:** Both Chartered Accountants and clients can access financial data remotely using mobile apps, fostering better collaboration for geographically dispersed teams or clients who travel frequently.

By leveraging these benefits, cloud accounting empowers Chartered Accountants to build stronger, more collaborative, and trusting relationships with their clients. They can transition from transactional accountants to valued financial advisors, ultimately contributing to the success and growth of their clients' businesses.

7.3 Time and Cost Savings

Cloud accounting is a cost-effective solution that translates into both time and monetary savings for practicing Chartered Accountants. Key factors include:

Reduced Time Spent on Manual Tasks:

- **Automation:**

  Cloud accounting automates many repetitive tasks that Chartered Accountants traditionally performed manually, such as data entry, bank reconciliation, and report generation. This frees up valuable time that Chartered Accountants can dedicate to higher-value activities like financial analysis, tax planning, and client consulting.

- **Streamlined workflows:**

  Cloud-based platforms offer integrated workflows that eliminate the need for switching between different software programs and manually transferring data. This reduces the time spent on administrative tasks and improves overall efficiency.

Improved Scalability and Cost Efficiency:

- **Subscription-based model:** Cloud accounting eliminates the need for expensive upfront investments in software licenses and hardware infrastructure. Chartered Accountants can choose a subscription plan that scales with their client base, allowing them to pay only for the features they need. This is particularly beneficial for Chartered Accountants who are just starting out or have a fluctuating client workload.

- **Reduced IT burden:** Cloud providers handle software updates, maintenance, and data security, eliminating the need for Chartered Accountants to invest in IT staff or resources to manage their accounting infrastructure. This translates to significant cost savings in the long run.

Enhanced Collaboration and Communication:

- **Real-time access:** Real-time access to financial data for both Chartered Accountants and clients eliminates the need for time-consuming data exchanges or waiting for reports to be generated.

This fosters faster communication and quicker resolution of client inquiries.

- **Improved client portals:** Secure client portals within cloud platforms allow for efficient information sharing and collaboration. Clients can easily upload documents and access real-time financial information, reducing the need for in-person meetings or lengthy email exchanges.

Additional Time and Cost Savings Benefits:

- **Reduced paperwork:** Cloud accounting promotes a paperless environment, eliminating the need for physical document storage and retrieval. This saves time and reduces costs associated with paper-based accounting systems.

- **Improved accessibility:** Mobile apps allow Chartered Accountants to access client data and manage tasks on the go, reducing the time spent on administrative tasks and improving overall productivity.

Overall Impact:

- By saving time on manual tasks, streamlining workflows, and reducing IT overheads, cloud accounting allows Chartered Accountants to operate more efficiently and cost-effectively. This translates into increased profitability for their practices and the ability to deliver a higher standard of service to their clients.

- Here are some additional points to consider:

- Cloud accounting can improve client satisfaction by enabling Chartered Accountants to be more responsive and proactive in addressing client needs.

- The time saved through automation and improved workflows allows Chartered Accountants to take on more clients or expand their service offerings, ultimately leading to increased revenue potential.

- If you're a CA looking to improve your practice's efficiency and profitability, cloud accounting is a powerful tool to consider. It can not only save you time and money but also empower you to deliver a better service to your clients.

7.4 Business Growth Opportunities

Cloud accounting serves as a catalyst for business growth, opening up new opportunities for practicing Chartered Accountants. Cloud accounting empowers Chartered Accountants to unlock new business growth opportunities in several ways:

Expanding Service Offerings:

- **Higher-value services:** Cloud accounting frees up Chartered Accountants' time from manual tasks, allowing them to focus on providing higher-value services to clients. This can include financial analysis, tax planning, business consulting, and strategic financial advising. By leveraging the data and insights generated by cloud platforms, Chartered Accountants can provide clients with more comprehensive financial guidance and help them make informed business decisions.

- **Specialized services:** Cloud accounting can open doors to specializing in niche areas. With more time available, Chartered Accountants can delve deeper into specific industries or develop expertise in areas like cloud-based financial modelling or data analytics. This specialization can attract new clients seeking tailored financial services.

Attracting New Clients:

- **Improved scalability:** Cloud-based solutions can easily scale to accommodate a growing practice. Chartered Accountants can take on more clients without worrying about infrastructure limitations associated with traditional on-premise accounting software. This allows them to expand their client base and reach new markets.

- **Enhanced client satisfaction:** The efficiency, transparency, and proactive financial guidance enabled by cloud accounting lead to higher client satisfaction. This translates to stronger client relationships, increased client retention, and the potential for referrals. Satisfied clients are more likely to recommend a CA to their network, leading to organic business growth.

- **Modern and tech-savvy image:** Adopting cloud accounting showcases a Chartered Accountants commitment to innovation and technology. This can be particularly appealing to younger businesses and entrepreneurs who value efficiency and accessibility.

Improved Efficiency and Profitability:

- **Reduced overhead costs:** Cloud accounting eliminates the need for upfront software purchases, server maintenance, and IT support staff. These cost savings can be reinvested in marketing, client service initiatives, or expanding the practice's service offerings.

- **Increased productivity:** Automation, streamlined workflows, and improved collaboration features within cloud platforms lead to increased productivity for Chartered Accountants and their staff. This allows them to accomplish more in less time, take on additional clients, and ultimately grow their revenue potential.

Here are some additional points to consider:

- **Cloud accounting fosters better communication and collaboration with clients.** This can lead to stronger client relationships and a deeper understanding of their financial needs, opening doors to new service opportunities.

- **Mobile accessibility allows Chartered Accountants to be more responsive to client needs.** This can improve client satisfaction and potentially lead to increased client engagement and recurring revenue streams through subscription-based services.

By leveraging the capabilities of cloud accounting, Chartered Accountants can not only improve their practice's efficiency and profitability but also unlock new avenues for business growth. They can expand their service offerings, attract new clients, and build a more successful and sustainable practice in the long run.

8

Case Studies

In this chapter, we delve into real-world Case Studies that highlight the success stories of firms that have adopted cloud accounting. We explore the benefits experienced by these firms, the challenges they faced during implementation, and the innovative solutions they implemented to overcome obstacles.

8.1 Success Stories of Firms Adopting Cloud Accounting

Case Study 1: TechFin Solutions

Background: TechFin Solutions, a tech-focused accounting firm based in Bangalore, transitioned to cloud accounting to align with its innovative approach to financial management.

Success Story:

- *Real-time Collaboration:* Cloud accounting allowed TechFin Solutions to collaborate with clients in real-time, facilitating quick decision-making and a more proactive advisory role.

- *Automation and Efficiency:* The firm experienced a significant reduction in manual data entry and reconciliation efforts. Automation of routine tasks increased operational efficiency by 40%, enabling the team to focus on strategic financial planning.

- *Global Reach:* TechFin expanded its client base globally, leveraging the accessibility and mobility offered by cloud accounting. This resulted in new opportunities and increased revenue streams.

Case Study 2: Progressive Accountancy Services

Background: Progressive Accountancy Services, a medium-sized firm in Mumbai, adopted cloud accounting to modernize its practices and stay competitive in the evolving financial landscape.

Success Story:

- *Enhanced Client Relationships:* Cloud accounting strengthened client relationships by providing clients with real-time insights into their financial data. This led to improved client satisfaction and loyalty.

- *Scalability:* Progressive Accountancy Services experienced a 25% increase in its client base without a proportional increase in operational costs. The scalability of cloud accounting allowed the firm to handle growth efficiently.

- *Competitive Advantage:* The adoption of cloud accounting positioned the firm as an innovative and forward-thinking service provider, giving it a competitive edge in the market.

8.2 Challenges Faced and Solutions Implemented

Case Study 3: Dynamic Accounting Solutions

Background: Dynamic Accounting Solutions, a small accounting firm in Chennai, faced challenges during its transition to cloud accounting.

Challenges:

- *Resistance to Change:* Some senior staff members were initially resistant to the shift to cloud accounting due to concerns about technology adoption and changes to established workflows.

- *Data Migration Complexity:* The process of migrating existing data to the cloud proved more complex than anticipated, leading to initial delays.

Solutions Implemented:

- *Change Management Initiatives:* Dynamic Accounting Solutions implemented change management workshops to address staff concerns and highlight the long-term benefits of cloud accounting. This improved acceptance and enthusiasm among the team.

- *Collaboration with Cloud Provider:* The firm engaged closely with the support team of the chosen cloud accounting platform to address data migration challenges. Regular communication and collaboration ensured a smoother transition.

By examining these Case studies, Chartered Accountants can gain valuable insights into the practical benefits of cloud accounting and learn from the experiences of their peers. Additionally, understanding the challenges faced and the innovative solutions implemented can provide guidance for a successful transition to cloud-based financial management.

9

Regulatory Compliance and Security Concerns

In the realm of cloud accounting, adherence to regulatory compliance and robust security measures is paramount. This chapter explores the specific considerations related to regulatory compliance and security concerns in the context of cloud accounting for practicing Chartered Accountants in India.

9.1 Data Protection and Privacy Laws in India

India, like many other jurisdictions, has stringent data protection and privacy laws designed to safeguard individuals' sensitive information. As Chartered Accountants transition to cloud accounting, compliance with these laws is crucial. Key considerations include:

Key Data Protection and Privacy Laws in India:

- **The Information Technology Act, 2000 (IT Act) and its Amendments:**

o This act establishes the legal framework for data protection and privacy in India. It outlines requirements for:

- **Data Ownership:** Defines ownership of data generated in electronic form.

- **User Consent:** Mandates obtaining user consent for collecting, storing, processing, and disclosing personal data.

- **Sensitive Personal Data (SPD):** Defines specific categories of data like passwords, financial information, and health records that require stricter consent and security measures.

- **Data Security Practices:** Emphasizes the need for reasonable security practices to protect personal data from unauthorized access, use, disclosure, or modification.

The Digital Personal Data Protection Act, 2023 (DPDP Act):

- This recently enacted law is the first comprehensive data protection legislation in India. It builds upon the IT Act and introduces stricter regulations on data processing, including:

  - **Purpose Limitation:** Personal data can only be processed for specific, clear, and lawful purposes.

  - **Right to be Forgotten:** Individuals have the right to request deletion of their personal data under certain circumstances.

  - **Data Localization Requirements:** While not a blanket data localization law, the DPDP Act empowers the government to mandate the storage of certain categories of data within India. This may have implications for cloud accounting service providers, and Chartered Accountants need to stay updated on any relevant regulations.

- **Cross-border Data Transfers:** The DPDP Act outlines procedures for transferring personal data outside India.

Compliance for Chartered Accountants using Cloud Accounting:

- **Understanding Client Data:** Identify the types of personal data you collect from clients and classify them as per the IT Act and DPDP Act (e.g., name, address, financial information). This helps determine the level of consent and security measures required.

- **Client Consent:** Obtain clear and informed consent from clients for collecting, storing, processing, and disclosing their personal data. The DPDP Act mandates specific requirements for consent forms, ensuring transparency and user control over their data.

- **Data Security Measures:** Choose a cloud accounting provider with robust security practices aligned with the IT Act and DPDP Act. Look for features like encryption, access controls, and regular security audits.

- **Data Breach Notification:** In case of a data breach, promptly notify your clients and the relevant authorities as mandated by the IT Act.

- **Record Keeping:** Maintain records of your data collection practices, consent obtained, and data breach incidents (if any) for potential audits by regulatory bodies.

Additional Considerations:

- **Professional Code of Conduct:** The Institute of Chartered Accountants of India (ICAI) Code of Ethics requires Chartered Accountants to maintain client confidentiality and data security. Cloud accounting practices should adhere to these ethical guidelines.

- **Staying Updated:** The data protection landscape in India is evolving. Regularly update yourself on changes to the IT Act, DPDP Act, and relevant regulations to ensure ongoing compliance.

By understanding the legal framework and implementing best practices, Chartered Accountants can navigate cloud accounting in India while safeguarding client data and upholding ethical standards. Remember, data protection and privacy are not just legal obligations but also essential for building trust with your clients.

9.2 Compliance with GST and Other Tax Regulations

India's complex tax landscape, particularly the Goods and Services Tax (GST), requires meticulous compliance from Chartered Accountants. When utilizing cloud accounting platforms, considerations for compliance with GST and other tax regulations include:

Streamlined GST Compliance:

- **Automated GST Calculations:** Cloud accounting software can automate GST calculations on invoices and purchases, reducing manual errors and saving Chartered Accountants valuable time.

- **GST Return Filing:** Many cloud platforms offer integrated features for filing GST returns electronically, eliminating manual data entry and streamlining the filing process.

- **Data Reconciliation:** Cloud-based systems facilitate easy reconciliation of GST data between invoices, purchases, and bank statements, ensuring accuracy in tax calculations and filings.

- **Audit Trail Maintenance:** Cloud accounting maintains a complete audit trail of all transactions, simplifying record-keeping and providing a clear picture for tax audits.

Compliance with Other Tax Regulations:

- **Income Tax (IT) Filings:** Cloud accounting software can help with income tax calculations, expense categorization, and generating reports relevant for IT return filing.

- **Tax Deducted at Source (TDS) Management:**

  Some platforms automate TDS calculations and filing procedures, reducing the risk of errors and penalties.

- **Data Integration with Tax Authorities:** Certain cloud providers offer integration with Indian tax authorities' portals, simplifying data submission and potentially expediting tax assessments.

Benefits for Chartered Accountants:

- **Improved Efficiency:**

  Automation and streamlined workflows free up Chartered Accountants' time for higher-value tasks like tax planning, strategy development, and client communication.

- **Reduced Errors:**

  Automating calculations and eliminating manual data entry significantly reduces errors in tax filings, minimizing the risk of penalties.

- **Enhanced Data Security:**

  Cloud platforms offer robust security features to safeguard sensitive financial data, ensuring compliance with data privacy regulations.

- **Real-time Insights:**

  Chartered Accountants can access real-time financial data and reports, allowing for proactive tax planning and informed decision-making throughout the year.

Additional Considerations:

- **Choosing a GST-compliant platform:** Ensure your chosen cloud accounting software is compliant with GST regulations and integrates seamlessly with the GST Network (GSTN) portal in India.

- **Chartered Accountant's Responsibility:** While cloud accounting automates tasks, Chartered Accountants still hold ultimate responsibility for ensuring accurate tax calculations and filings. Thorough review and professional judgment remain crucial.

- **Staying Updated:** The Indian tax landscape is subject to change. Chartered Accountants need to stay updated on revisions to GST regulations and other tax laws to ensure their cloud accounting practices remain compliant.

By leveraging the functionalities of cloud accounting platforms, Chartered Accountants can navigate the complexities of GST and other tax regulations in India more efficiently and accurately. This allows them to focus on higher-value services for their clients while minimizing the risk of errors and penalties.

9.3 Ensuring Data Security and Client Confidentiality

Security concerns, including data breaches and unauthorized access, are top priorities when dealing with financial information. Practicing Chartered Accountants must implement robust security measures to ensure data security and client confidentiality.

Choosing a Secure Cloud Provider:

- **Security Certifications:** *Look for providers with certifications like SOC 2 and ISO 27001, demonstrating their commitment to data security best practices.*

- **Data Encryption:** *Ensure the provider encrypts data at rest (stored data) and in transit (data being transferred) using industry-standard encryption protocols like AES 256-bit.*

- **Access Controls:** *Choose a platform offering multi-factor authentication (MFA) and granular access controls. MFA adds an extra layer of security by* *requiring a second verification factor beyond just a username and password. Granular access controls allow you to restrict user access to specific data sets based on their roles and responsibilities.*

- **Data Residency:** *Consider where your client data will be stored. If there are any data residency restrictions in your jurisdiction, choose a provider with data storage options that comply with those regulations.*

- **Disaster Recovery and Backups:** *Ensure the provider has a robust disaster recovery plan and regularly backs up data to ensure information remains safe in Case Studies of unforeseen events.*

Implementing Secure Practices in Your Firm:

- **Data Minimization:** *Collect only the client data essential for your services. Limiting the amount of data stored minimizes the potential impact of a security breach.*

- **_Strong Password Policies:_** _Enforce strong password policies for all user accounts, including your own and your clients'. Encourage the use of password managers to generate and store complex passwords securely._

- **_Regular User Activity Monitoring:_** _Monitor user activity logs to identify any suspicious behavior that might indicate unauthorized access attempts._

- **_Data Security Training:_** _Educate your staff on data security best practices, including password hygiene, phishing awareness, and the importance of reporting suspicious activity._

Maintaining Client Trust:

- **_Client Communication:_** _Communicate your data security measures to your clients. This transparency builds trust and demonstrates your commitment to safeguarding their confidential information._

- **_Contractual Agreements:_** _Ensure your contracts with clients outline data security responsibilities, including breach notification procedures._

Additional Considerations:

- ***Staying Updated:*** *The cyber threat landscape is constantly evolving. Stay informed about emerging threats and update your security practices accordingly.*

- ***Regular Security Audits:*** *Conduct periodic security audits of your cloud accounting environment to identify and address any potential vulnerabilities.*

By prioritizing these strategies, Chartered Accountants can establish robust security measures for their cloud accounting practices. Remember, data security is an ongoing process, not a one-time fix. Vigilance and continuous improvement are key to maintaining client confidentiality and trust in the digital age.

Future Trends and Developments

As technology continues to evolve, the future of cloud accounting holds exciting possibilities that will reshape the landscape for practicing Chartered Accountants. This chapter explores emerging trends and developments, including the integration of AI and automation, the role of blockchain, and the changing dynamics of the accounting profession.

10.1 AI and Automation in Cloud Accounting

10.1.1 Intelligent Automation: The integration of Artificial Intelligence (AI) and automation into cloud accounting platforms is set to revolutionize how financial data is processed and analyzed. Intelligent automation can handle routine tasks, such as data entry and categorization, with unprecedented speed and accuracy. This enables Chartered Accountants to focus on high-value activities such as strategic advisory services, financial planning, and decision-making.

10.1.2 Predictive Analytics: AI-driven predictive analytics will play a crucial role in forecasting financial trends, identifying potential risks, and providing valuable insights for businesses. Cloud accounting platforms will leverage machine learning algorithms to analyze historical data, enabling Chartered Accountants to offer more proactive and data-driven advice to their clients.

10.1.3 Personalized Financial Insights: AI algorithms will enable cloud accounting systems to deliver personalized financial insights to clients. From expense optimization suggestions to investment strategies, these platforms will become intelligent assistants, empowering both Chartered Accountants and their clients to make informed financial decisions.

10.2 Blockchain Integration

10.2.1 Enhanced Security and Transparency: The integration of blockchain technology into cloud accounting platforms will provide an extra layer of security and transparency. Blockchain's decentralized and tamper-resistant ledger can ensure the integrity of financial transactions, reducing the risk of fraud and enhancing trust in the financial data stored on the cloud.

10.2.2 Smart Contracts for Automation: Smart contracts, powered by blockchain, can automate financial processes within the cloud accounting ecosystem. This includes automating invoicing, payment processing, and compliance tasks. The immutability of smart contracts ensures that transactions are executed transparently and without the need for intermediaries.

10.2.3 Streamlining Audit Processes: Blockchain's traceability and transparency features can streamline audit processes. Auditors can access an unchangeable record of financial transactions, reducing the time and resources required for audits while enhancing accuracy and trust in financial reporting.

10.3 Changing Dynamics of the Accounting Profession

10.3.1 Evolving Roles of Chartered Accountants: The adoption of cloud accounting, AI, and automation will redefine the roles of Chartered Accountants. Chartered Accountants will transition from traditional bookkeeping roles to becoming strategic advisors, leveraging technology to offer more value-added services. Skills such as data analysis, interpretation, and strategic planning will become increasingly crucial.

10.3.2 Collaborative Ecosystems: Cloud accounting platforms will foster collaborative ecosystems, connecting Chartered Accountants, clients, and other stakeholders seamlessly. This interconnectedness will enhance communication, enable real-time collaboration, and create an ecosystem where financial information flows seamlessly across various platforms and applications.

10.3.3 Continued Professional Development: The changing dynamics of the accounting profession will necessitate continuous professional development for Chartered Accountants. Staying abreast of technological advancements, regulatory changes, and emerging trends will be imperative for professionals to remain competitive and provide high-quality services.

As the future unfolds, the convergence of cloud accounting with AI, automation, and blockchain promises a transformative journey for Chartered Accountants. Embracing these trends will not only enhance efficiency and accuracy but will position Chartered Accountants as indispensable strategic partners in the financial success of their clients.

11

Conclusion

In conclusion, the journey through the realms of cloud accounting in the Indian landscape has unveiled a transformative path for practicing Chartered Accountants. As we recap the key points explored in this comprehensive guide, delve into the future trends, and issue a call to action, it becomes evident that the intersection of technology and accounting holds immense potential for growth, efficiency, and innovation.

11.1 Recap of Key Points

Throughout this exploration, we've navigated the landscape of cloud accounting, understanding its definition, evolution, advantages, and challenges. We delved into the current state of accounting in India, recognizing the traditional practices and the pressing need for technological integration. Key features of popular cloud accounting platforms were examined, offering insights into the tools that can revolutionize accounting practices.

Implementing cloud accounting in practice requires a strategic approach, encompassing steps for transition, overcoming resistance, and prioritizing training and skill development. The benefits for practicing Chartered Accountants are substantial, including improved efficiency, enhanced client relationships, and significant time and cost savings.

Case studies illuminated success stories and the innovative solutions adopted by firms, providing tangible examples for Chartered Accountants considering the transition. Regulatory compliance and security concerns took center stage, emphasizing the importance of aligning with data protection laws, ensuring GST compliance, and implementing robust security measures.

11.2 The Future of Cloud Accounting in India

Looking ahead, the future of cloud accounting in India is poised for continued evolution. The integration of AI and automation promises to revolutionize accounting processes, enhancing efficiency and accuracy. Blockchain integration introduces new possibilities for secure, transparent, and tamper-proof financial transactions.

The dynamics of the accounting profession are shifting, with cloud accounting emerging as a catalyst for change. The role of Chartered Accountants is expanding beyond traditional compliance services to strategic advisory roles, providing insights and guidance to clients for informed decision-making.

The future of cloud accounting in India is bright and brimming with exciting possibilities. Here's a glimpse into what we can expect:

Growing Adoption:

- **Increased Awareness and Benefits:** As Chartered Accountants and businesses become more aware of the benefits of cloud accounting, adoption is likely to accelerate across all sectors.

- **Government Initiatives:** The Indian government's focus on digital transformation might include initiatives promoting cloud adoption for small and medium businesses (SMBs), further propelling the growth of cloud accounting.

Evolving Technologies:

- **Advanced AI and Automation:** AI will become even more sophisticated, automating complex tasks like financial forecasting, risk assessment, and audit preparation. This will free up Chartered Accountants' time for even more strategic client service.

- **Integration with Fintech and Business Applications:** Cloud accounting platforms will seamlessly integrate with a wider range of fintech and business applications, such as payment gateways, e-invoicing systems, and customer relationship management (CRM) software. This will create a more holistic financial ecosystem for businesses.

Focus on Security and Compliance:

- **Enhanced Security Features:** Cloud providers will continue to develop robust security features to address evolving cyber threats and maintain the highest level of data security for client information.

- **Regulatory Alignment:** Cloud accounting solutions will adapt and integrate seamlessly with

India's evolving data privacy and tax regulations, such as the DPDP Act and GST requirements.

Shifting CA Roles and Services:

- **Advisory and Strategic Focus:** With automation handling routine tasks, Chartered Accountants will transition to a more advisory role. They will focus on providing strategic financial planning, business consulting, and leveraging AI-powered insights to help clients make informed business decisions.

- **Specialization and Niche Services:** Chartered Accountants might specialize in specific industries or leverage their expertise in AI and data analysis to offer niche services like cloud-based financial modeling or data-driven financial consulting.

Overall Impact:

The future of cloud accounting in India promises a more efficient, data-driven, and secure financial management landscape for businesses. Chartered Accountants will play a pivotal role in this ecosystem, acting as trusted advisors and leveraging technology to empower their clients for success.

Here are some additional points to consider:

- **The rise of cloud-based accounting solutions will likely lead to increased competition among providers.** This will benefit Chartered Accountants and businesses by offering a wider range of options with competitive pricing and features.

- **The increasing adoption of cloud accounting might create new job opportunities for Chartered Accountants with expertise in cloud technologies and data analysis.**

- **The continuous development of cloud accounting solutions will necessitate continuous learning for Chartered Accountants.** Staying updated on the latest advancements and upskilling in relevant areas will be crucial for success in the future.

By embracing cloud accounting and its evolving functionalities, Chartered Accountants in India can position themselves as valuable strategic partners for their clients and navigate the exciting future of the accounting profession.

11.3 Call to Action for Practicing Chartered Accountants

The landscape of accounting in India is undergoing a transformative shift. Cloud accounting, with its unparalleled efficiency, security, and data-driven insights, is rapidly becoming the new standard. For Chartered Accountants in India, this presents a pivotal moment – a crossroads where tradition meets innovation. The call to action is clear: embrace cloud accounting and unlock its transformative potential.

Embrace Change: Reimagine the Future of Accounting

For generations, Chartered Accountants have relied on established practices. However, clinging to the familiar can hinder progress. Cloud accounting offers a powerful leap forward, streamlining workflows, automating mundane tasks, and providing real-time access to financial data. It's time to shed the inhibitions of the past and embrace the transformative power of this technology.

Invest in Technology: Find the Perfect Cloud Fit

The cloud accounting landscape is brimming with options. It's crucial to choose a platform that seamlessly integrates with your existing workflows and caters to your specific needs. Explore different solutions, consider client requirements, and prioritize features like data security, scalability, and integration capabilities. Investing in the right cloud platform is an investment in the future of your practice.

Prioritize Training: Empower Yourself and Your Team

Cloud accounting unlocks a world of new possibilities. However, maximizing its potential requires a skilled workforce. Prioritize training for yourself and your team. Equip them with the knowledge and expertise to navigate the platform, utilize its features effectively, and leverage its data-driven insights. Consider various training options, from online courses offered by cloud providers to workshops conducted by industry experts. A well-trained team is crucial for a successful cloud accounting transition.

Stay Informed: Navigate the Evolving Landscape

The world of accounting is constantly evolving. Regulatory frameworks adapt, security best practices are refined, and new technologies emerge. To ensure compliance and stay relevant, commit to continuous learning. Actively follow industry publications, attend seminars on cloud accounting and data security, and network with fellow Chartered Accountants to stay abreast of the latest trends. A proactive approach to knowledge gathering will ensure your practice stays ahead of the curve.

Position Yourself Strategically: From Compliance to Value-Added Services

Cloud accounting automates routine tasks, freeing up valuable time for Chartered Accountants to shift their focus. Move beyond mere compliance and position yourself as a strategic advisor. Leverage the data and insights generated by cloud platforms to provide clients with proactive financial guidance, identify growth opportunities, and develop data-driven business strategies. This shift in focus will solidify your position as a trusted advisor, creating an invaluable partnership with your clients.

Beyond the Call: Embracing a Culture of Innovation

The call to action goes beyond simply adopting cloud accounting. It's about fostering a culture of innovation within your practice. Explore the potential of AI and automation within cloud platforms. Consider offering niche services built on your expertise in cloud technology and data analysis. Actively seek out opportunities to collaborate with other professionals, like fintech startups, to deliver a holistic financial experience for your clients. By embracing innovation, you'll not only enhance your own practice but contribute to the advancement of the accounting profession in India.

The Road Ahead: A Collaborative Journey

The transition to cloud accounting is not a solitary endeavor. Collaboration and knowledge sharing are key. Partner with your clients, educate them on the benefits of cloud accounting, and work together to leverage its capabilities. Additionally, connect with other Chartered Accountants who have successfully adopted cloud technology. Share experiences, learn from their journeys, and build a network of like-minded professionals. This collaborative approach will pave the way for a smoother transition and create a stronger, more informed community of Chartered Accountants in India.

Embrace the Future Today: A Legacy of Growth and Success

The future of accounting in India belongs to those who embrace change. By adopting cloud accounting, Chartered Accountants can enhance their practices, empower their clients, and contribute significantly to the growth of Indian businesses. This is an opportunity to build a legacy – a legacy built on innovation, efficiency, and a commitment to providing exceptional financial services. The journey begins today. Take the first step, embrace cloud accounting, and unlock the limitless potential it offers for your practice and the future of accounting in India.

Appendix

Glossary of Terms

1. **Cloud Accounting:** The practice of using web-based accounting software to perform accounting tasks, manage financial data, and collaborate with clients in real-time.

2. **GST (Goods and Services Tax):** A comprehensive indirect tax levied on the supply of goods and services in India, replacing multiple indirect taxes.

3. **Automation:** The use of technology to perform tasks and processes with minimal human intervention, enhancing efficiency and reducing manual effort.

4. **Data Encryption:** The process of converting data into a code to prevent unauthorized access, ensuring the confidentiality and security of sensitive information.

5. **Change Management:** A structured approach to transitioning individuals, teams, and organizations

from a current state to a desired future state, especially when implementing new technologies.

6. **Blockchain:** A decentralized and distributed ledger technology that ensures secure and transparent record-keeping of transactions through a chain of blocks.

7. **AI (Artificial Intelligence):** The simulation of human intelligence in machines, enabling them to perform tasks that typically require human intelligence, such as learning and problem-solving.

8. **Compliance:** Adherence to laws, regulations, and industry standards to ensure that business practices are ethical, legal, and in line with applicable requirements.

CA. PEEYUSH SHARMA, FCA, DISA(ICAI)

Professional Profile: Peeyush Sharma is a distinguished Chartered Accountant, holding the esteemed designation of Fellow Chartered Accountant (FCA) and certified in Information Systems Audit (DISA) by the Institute of Chartered Accountants of India (ICAI). With a career spanning nearly two decades, Sharma has excelled as a practicing Chartered Accountant since 2005.

Education and Credentials:

- Fellow Chartered Accountant (FCA) from ICAI

- Information Systems Audit (DISA) from ICAI

Experience: Peeyush Sharma boasts profound expertise in financial management, taxation, and information systems. With a focus on delivering comprehensive financial advisory services, he caters to a diverse clientele, including individuals, corporations, and non-profit organizations.

Areas of Expertise:

1. Taxation: Sharma provides strategic tax planning and compliance services, adeptly navigating both national and international tax regulations.

2. Financial Management: With a sharp acumen for financial analysis, budgeting, and forecasting, Sharma assists clients in making informed decisions to foster sustainable financial growth.

3. Information Systems Audit: Holding the DISA certification from ICAI, Sharma specializes in evaluating and fortifying the effectiveness of

information systems, ensuring the implementation of robust internal controls and data security measures.

Professional Involvement: An active member of the Institute of Chartered Accountants of India (ICAI), Peeyush Sharma remains dedicated to the advancement of the accounting profession. He stays abreast of industry developments and contributes to its evolution.

Commitment to Excellence: Peeyush Sharma is renowned for his unwavering commitment to excellence and adherence to ethical business practices. He delivers tailored solutions that precisely align with the unique needs of his clients. Sharma's professional demeanor, coupled with meticulous attention to detail, has solidified his reputable standing in the fields of accounting and finance.

CA. Peeyush Sharma, FCA, DISA (ICA)
peeyushsharmaca@gmail.com